A Guide to Fishing and Boating
on the Norfolk and Suffolk Broads

A Guide to Fishing and Boating on the Norfolk and Suffolk Broads

PETER CRAVEN

© Peter Craven, 2014

Published by Peter Craven

First Published 2014

2nd Revised Edition 2018

A CIP catalogue record for this book is available from the British Library.

ISBN 978-0-9931402-0-4

Book layout and design by Clare Brayshaw

Cover design by David Batten with thanks to Gail Sparks

Prepared and printed by:

York Publishing Services Ltd
64 Hallfield Road
Layerthorpe
York YO31 7ZQ

Tel: 01904 431213

Website: www.yps-publishing.co.uk

Dedication

To Sarah without who's company the river would not have been quite so blue, or the trees quite as green.

Reviews for the First Edition

"This light hearted yet highly informative book covers all aspects of fishing and boating on the broads."

Coarse Fishing Today magazine review June 2015.

"Retailing at only £9.99 this guide is worth much more in terms of the information provided and would be ideal for anyone looking to explore the broads."

Pike and Predator Magazine June 2015

"A must read for broads holidays."

Angling Times July 21st 2015

Contents

Acknowledgements

Maps – Anthony Graham (Illustrative maps)

Fishing Illustrations – David Batten (Hooklinks)

Original Cover Photo – "Roll on Spring" by Gail Sparks

Cover design and arrangement – David Batten (Hooklinks)

Typing and corrections – Sarah Richards

Graphics Assistant – Charlotte O'Hara

Serene Gem photo – Chris Kirk

Key to maps

Rivers / Broads		End of navigation	
Mooring bollard		Kingfisher	
Pike		Geese	
Bream		Trees	
Silverfish		Marsh Harrier	
Perch		Oystercatcher	
Eel		Goosander	
Boatyard		Cormorant	
Reedbeds		Otter	
Cattle		Rhododendrons	
Good pub		Foxgloves	
Bridge			
Low bridge			

Introduction

Thanks for giving the book a go and I hope you enjoy it. It's split into three sections, the first has maps of the Broads Rivers. The Broads rivers themselves vary a great deal in their character – from tree lined meandering river sections with kingfishers diving from branches, to vast open reed beds with marsh harriers wheeling slow overhead. Then there are mudflats picked over by wading birds and the town and village sections with gardens running down to the river. I try to capture the flavour of these different parts of the Broads.

Section 2 is the fishing one, however it's not a specialist fishing book and I have pitched it at someone who is new to the Broads but does a bit of fishing for fun. If fishing is just not your thing then this is probably not the section for you.

The boating section is aimed at the complete novice. Experienced boaters and boat owners will find it all a bit basic, but for those new to the wet stuff I hope it answers a few questions about how to drive and moor boats – as well as a few safety points.

The broads are a wonderful place very close to my own heart and I hope that you enjoy reading the book as I have very much enjoyed writing it.

CHAPTER 1

A guide to the Norfolk and Suffolk Broads

The North Broads

N

Great Yarmouth
Yarmouth/Acle Road Bridge
Breydon Water

Norwich

Cottishall

River Bure

Wroxham
Wroxham Bridge
Hoveton
Hoveton Little Broad
Wroxham Broad
Hoveton Great Broad
Salhouse Broad

Horning
Cockshoot Broad
Ranworth & Malthouse Broads
Ranworth

Neatishead

Barton Turf

Wayford Bridge
Dilham Dyke
Stalham Dyke
Stalham
Sutton Broad
Sutton
How Hill
Barton Broad
River Ant

Ludham
Ludham Bridge
Ant mouth

South Walsham
South Walsham Broad
Fleet Dyke

Upton
Upton Dyke

Acle
Acle Bridge
Acle Dyke

Stokesby

River Bure

Hickling
Hickling Broad
Hickling Staithe

Potter Heigham
Old Bridge
New Bridge
Womack Water

West Somerton
Martham
Martham Broad

Horsey
Horsey Mere
Winterton Dunes

Waxham New Cut

River Thurne
Thurne
Thurne mouth
Thurne Dyke

2

The South Norfolk and Suffolk Broads

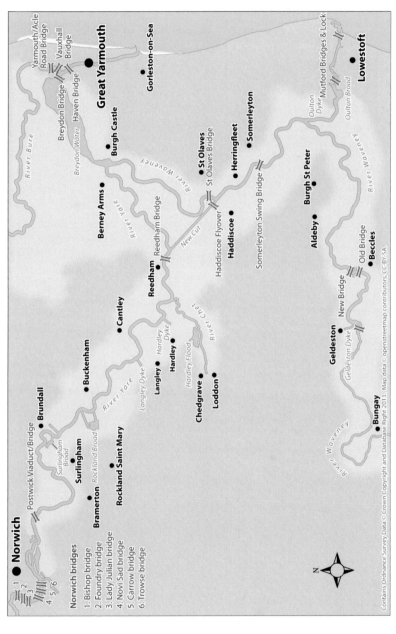

Norwich

Postwick Viaduct/Bridge

Norwich bridges
1. Bishop bridge
2. Foundry bridge
3. Lady Julian bridge
4. Novi Sad bridge
5. Carrow bridge
6. Trowse bridge

Brundall

Surlingham
Surlingham Broad

Bramerton

Rockland Broad

Rockland Saint Mary

Buckenham

Cantley

River Yare

Langley Dyke

Langley
Hardley Dyke
Hardley
Hardley Flood

Chedgrave
Loddon

River Chet

Reedham

Reedham Bridge

New Cut

Berney Arms

River Yare

Breydon Water

Breydon Bridge
Haven Bridge

Great Yarmouth

Yarmouth/Acle Road Bridge
Vauxhall Bridge

Gorleston-on-Sea

Burgh Castle

River Bure

River Waveney

St Olaves
St Olaves Bridge

Haddiscoe Flyover

Haddiscoe

Somerleyton Swing Bridge

Herringfleet

Somerleyton

Burgh St Peter

Aldeby

Geldeston
Geldeston Dyke

New Bridge

Old Bridge
Beccles

Bungay

River Waveney

Oulton Dyke

Mutford Bridges & Lock

Oulton Broad

Lowestoft

N

The River Ant

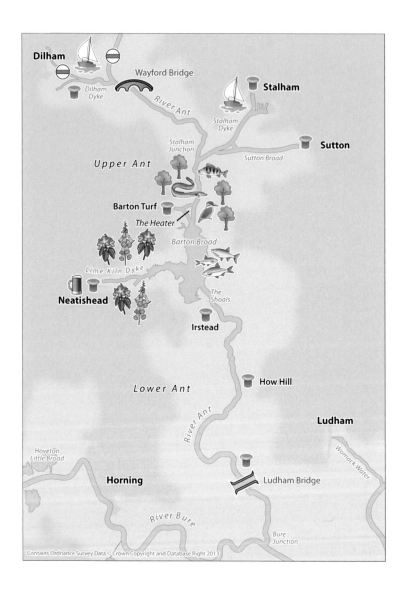

Dilham

Wayford Bridge

Dilham Dyke

River Ant

Stalham

Stalham Dyke

Stalham Junction

Sutton

Sutton Broad

Upper Ant

Barton Turf

The Heater

Barton Broad

Lime Kiln Dyke

Neatishead

The Shoals

Irstead

How Hill

Lower Ant

Ludham

River Ant

Womack Water

Hoveton Little Broad

Horning

Ludham Bridge

River Bure

Bure Junction

Contains Ordnance Survey Data © Crown Copyright and Database Right 2013

The Hoseasons yard at Stalham is probably the biggest boatyard on the broads and consequently the Upper Ant and the run up to Stalham can carry a lot of boat traffic at times. This is particularly true on Friday's when people start to head up the Ant to return their boats on a Saturday morning, with the return traffic from the re-hired boats running in the opposite direction in the afternoon. Therefore if you want a slightly quieter time on the way up to Stalham mid-week is probably the best bet.

Just along from Stalham is Sutton broad which gives the impression of a wide shallow expanse of river rather than what one would naturally think of as a broad. There are limited moorings at Sutton. As with all of the upper Ant system this section is not particularly tidal and meanders gently between tree lined banks, it is what one might describe as a Kenneth Graham type river from his book Wind in the Willows with picturesque view followed by picturesque view around each bend – ah well another lousy day in paradise. The run from Barton broad to Stalham must also be one of the best places on the broads for kingfishers and on this particular stretch those iridescent flashes of turquoise are a common sight.

Turning right at Stalham junction up to Wayford Bridge it soon narrows to the point where it is not really suited to the larger cruisers and Wayford Bridge marks the navigable limit of the Upper Ant for most. Running down from Wayford Bridge to Stalham Junction and beyond is a pleasant mix between the more open reed lined banks so typical of the broads in general and the picturesque tree lined banks of the Upper Ant. In the end the tree lined paradise of the Upper Ant wins out and the sheer rivery charm of this section is quite overwhelming with secluded overnight moorings for a single boat hitched to a willow tree or tethered on land anchors, ten a penny on this stretch.

One side effect however of this tree lined haven are the midges which in hot still weather tuck into their favourite evening meal of tourist slightly pink. On hot still evenings it is definitely a place for keeping well covered and lathered in mosquito repellent. A mosquito hat or hood with a drop down gauze over the face may seem a bit excessive and look like a berka but really does work.

The fishing on this section is of a different character to the majority of the broads. The big bream shoals which are in many ways the hallmark of broads fishing are largely absent and perch are probably the dominant species of the Upper Ant.

Barton Broad and the Lower Ant down to the Bure Junction

Leaving the Upper Ant, Barton Broad is entered via the 'heater' end which is a short wedged shaped navigation leading off to the village of Barton Turf. Barton Broad itself is popular for sailing and can get crowded particularly at the weekend. That said there are some very pleasant quiet day moorings tucked into its tree lined banks. In recent years the broad has had much of the silt removed in the clear water project so your mud weight probably will not hold so well as on other broads. In fishing terms it is home to good shoals of silver fish particularly rudd.

On its western side Barton Broad narrows first into an inlet and then into Limekiln dyke which although tight for the larger cruisers is an absolute joy to navigate. In high summer it's wooded banks blaze brightly with rhododendrons and foxgloves. Once again a small stretch of narrow river located somewhere to the left hand side of paradise.

Leaving Barton Broad takes you through "the shoals" and into the lower Ant proper through the village of Irstead which like Wroxham provides a sort of millionaires row of reed thatched new builds whose gardens run down to their own private moorings. It is past these that one can observe the contrast between the lower and upper Ant as trees give way to at first reed beds and then dyke drained fields. This same contrast between the tree lined upper reaches of the broads rivers and their more agrian lower reaches of predominantly grassland with some arable is also a feature of the Bure and Waveny. When it comes to the Thurne the upper and lower reaches are indeed different although in this case the upper reaches are a land of reeds not trees.

There are a reasonable amount of free moorings on the Lower Ant around Howe Hill and later Ludham Bridge. As broads bridges go Ludham Bridge is not too bad to navigate being a relatively modern road bridge although the trick that it keeps up its sleeve, is that it is situated on a bend in the river which does reduce visibility. I have generally found fishing on the Lower Ant to be predominantly bream, roach and skimmer orientated and I would describe it as OK, but certainly not the cream of broads angling.

The Upper Bure

The Upper Bure has broads like Imelda Marcos had shoes. In order from Wroxham down to the mouth the Ant: Wroxham Broad, Hoveton Great Broad, Salhouse Broad, Decoy Broad, Hoveton Little Broad, Cockshoot Broad, Ranworth Broad, Malthouse Broad and South Walsham Broad.

One of the local boatyards calls this section of the Bure the M25 (Norfolk really does have its charm as the nearest thing that it has to a motorway is a stretch of idyllic river scattered with broads) However nicknaming the Upper Bure the M25 does indicate that it can get busy in summer.

The Upper Bure down to the Thurne Mouth

Cottishall

River Bure

Wroxham
Wroxham Bridge
Wroxham Broad

Hoveton
Hoveton Great Broad
Hoveton Little Broad

Salhouse
Salhouse Broad

Decoy Broad

Cockshoot Broad

Ranworth
Ranworth Broad
Malthouse Broad

South Walsham Broad

Horning

Irstead

River Ant

How Hill

Ludham

Ludham Bridge

Bure Junction

River Bure

Womack Water

River Thurne

Thurne Mouth

There are plenty of free moorings and the fishing is good but sometimes in the height of the season it does start to feel a bit like a caravan site on an August Bank Holiday. That said try the Upper Bure in October, when the cooling autumn air has thinned out the crowds and you can have the broads and moorings virtually to yourselves.

If the Upper Bure is the M25 of the broads then Wroxham is its capital. Both Wroxham and Horning have been subject to some fairly high class residential development, in the reed thatch, white wash, cobble and brick palette that goes to make up Norfolk's own distinctive vernacular architecture. I am reminded of a story I was told about the centre of Vancouver in Canada where some enterprising property tycoon had built a development of log cabins – high class log cabins I grant you, but log cabins all the same – and these had rapidly established themselves as some of the most desirable residences in the city.

Wroxham is also home to the Blakes boatyard which is one of the busiest on the Broads, it seems to specialise in the larger more modern cruisers. This can make Wroxham itself quite busy and although the railway bridge has plenty of clearance the bigger cruisers can struggle to pass under the lower road bridge, (there is a pilot service available) which does considerably reduce boat traffic on the Bure above Wroxham on the run up to Cottishall. Cottishall itself is a real delight with a good mooring and an excellent riverside pub.

The Thurne, Martham Broad, Horsey and Hickling

The run up from the Thurne mouth to Potter Heigham is pleasant enough with a couple of popular moorings off the river at Thurne itself and Ludham. As you come into Potter Heigham there is a long ribbon development of

The Thurne, Martham Broad, Horsey and Hickling

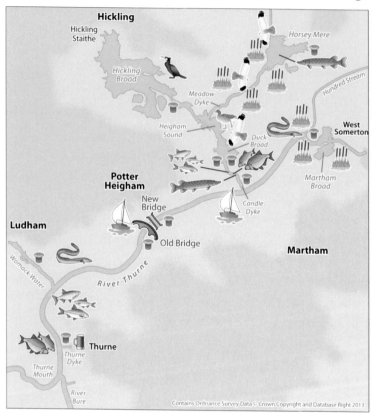

Contains Ordnance Survey Data © Crown Copyright and Database Right 2013

houses which are a bit like bungalows and a bit like seaside chalets, each with their own river frontage and mooring. In fact Potter Heigham although an inland broads village does always seem to have some shingle and sand caught in its hair and have a seaside feel about it.

At Potter Heigham you will come to the old arched stone road bridge. If you are in a big cruiser this is the end of the Thurne for you and you will have to either turn around or moor up. On the other hand if you are in a craft that can pass under the old arched bridge, then the upper Thurne is yours to enjoy. Private boats are permitted to navigate the old arch themselves. Hire boats have to moor up and let the pilot run them through. The next bridge is Potter Heigham new road bridge and at 7'9" in a normal tide it does give around an extra foot of headroom over the old bridge. Its span is bank to bank making it easy to navigate although that said it is still low enough to catch you out, particularly if you do not lower any screens and canopies on your boat.

The run up the Thurne to West Somerton takes you past candle dyke to which I shall return later and through Martham Broad. Just before Martham broad where Hundred Stream Drain joins the Thurne as it almost doubles back on itself, is one of my favourite moorings that fishes particularly well for eels. The Thurne is starting to narrow at this point and shallow up, the water is clear and the sunlight penetrating the water leads to fairly heavy weed growth on the upper Thurne.

Martham Broad itself is surrounded by what amounts to probably several hundred acres of reed beds and is managed as a nature reserve. There is a navigation channel through it which gives a good view of the broad and its bird life but the broad itself is not open to pleasure craft. The Thurne ends at West Somerton staith and in case I have not mentioned it before, a staith is simply a mooring usually associated with a village.

I referred to Candle Dyke a moment ago, that branches off the Thurne at Martham. Returning to this it provides access via Heigham sound to the very extensive broads system of Hickling and Horsey Mere. Dealing first with Candle dyke and Higham sound, there are plenty of really pleasant moorings on this section and the fishing is the absolute cream. In fact it fishes so well to conventional feeder tactics that you begin to wonder at the size of the bream, roach and hybrid shoals that it must contain.

At Heigham sound you can either turn off to Horsey or keep motoring into Hickling Broad. Hickling is a large expanse of water although much of it is off limits to hire craft. There is however a generous navigation through the broad which is both wide and well-marked with posts. The right fork at Heigham sound leads to Horsey Mere via Meadow Dyke. Horsey is particularly popular for sailing – probably a combination of it being a fair sized spit of open water and it nearly always having a sea breeze (being only about a mile from the coast). Oh and the way it looks of course. Simply stunning.

Before leaving Martham Broad, Horsey and Hickling it is perhaps worth taking a minute to consider them as a single system, as all three are surrounded by extensive reed beds which link them as a single reed and broad based habitat. It is perhaps partly due to this along with the policy of maintaining pockets of low disturbance refuge areas that contribute to it being such a haven for bird life.

There are extensive flocks of geese and other water fowl that patrol the Thurne and its broads. In fact the procession of waterfowl swimming past your moored boat in the morning can be so numerous as to seem like a steady stream of commuters on a city street.

The lone black cormorants in contrast sit hunched on any post that comes to hand. Their silhouettes against the sky or water looking about one third ugly, one third cool and one third sinister all at the same time. Again as with the pike if an area is packed with prey – and the upper Thurne system is packed to the gills with bite sized shoals of silver fish – then the hunters will come and in the case of cormorants, hang about on their posts for a bit looking for trouble or at least the next meal, which ever happens along first.

The grey herons however stand on one leg in the shallows – patient as all fishermen learn to be patient. Annoyed as all professional fishermen are annoyed if they are disturbed by the tourists. They rise slow and disdainful at the visitor who ruins the fishing and forces them to move to a new spot and what of the marsh harriers of the upper Thurne? Simply stunning as they wheel high or hunt low over the reed beds.

The Lower Bure

The Lower Bure from the Thurne mouth down takes you past Acle and Stokesby both large popular moorings, both with a really good pub on hand and both absolutely stacked to the gills with huge shoals of cracking bream. The skimmers, roach and hybrids may be a bit thinner on the ground in this section compared to the Thurne but to be quite honest they are probably just getting shouldered out by the gangs of heavy, humped backed thugs that pass themselves off as bream shoals. The Acle Stokesby section of the Bure runs fast and deep reminding me of the Lower Waveney around Somerleyton – no coincidence perhaps that big bream abound in both.

Once you get much past Stokesby there is no mooring on the run down to Great Yarmouth The fall between high and low tides on this stretch is considerable, revealing large sections of mud at low tide, much to the delight of the wading birds. As you approach Great Yarmouth the town gives the impression of being close at hand but then the river starts to twist and turn and hook round seeming to take you further not nearer to your destination.

Great Yarmouth has a number of bridges – often more narrow than low – and is subject to strong currents. This is particularly evident where the twin currents of the Lower

River Bure from the Thurne Mouth to Great Yarmouth

Thurne
Thurne Dyke
Thurne Mouth
Boundary House Staithe
Upton Marshes
Upton Dyke
Upton
Acle Dyke
Acle
Acle Bridge
Stokesby
Rollesby
Filby
California
Ormesby St Margaret
Caister-on-Sea
River Bure
South Walsham Marshes
Breydon Water
Great Yarmouth
Yarmouth/Acle Road Bridge
Vauxhall Bridge
Breydon Bridge
Haven Bridge

Contains Ordnance Survey Data © Crown Copyright and Database Right 2013

Bure and the Yare meet. By the way when you navigate the markers in Yarmouth coming from the Bure turn right into the south broads not left, as left is the North Sea, by all accounts this can get choppy at times and is not really suitable for hire craft. Do not worry it is clearly marked. For all of the above reasons – bridges, strong currents and not forgetting the North sea it is best to time your navigation of Great Yarmouth to coincide with slack water just after low tide.

The South Broads

Leaving Yarmouth you enter Breydon Water which is an extensive flood of several hundred acres. It is either water or mud depending on whether the tide is in or out. The deep central channel is well marked by metal posts which are numbered. Even at high water it is best not to venture out of the channel and onto the flats as you can run aground and be left high and dry. Always a bit of an embarrassment as you stand on deck and survey the scene – captain numpty who stranded himself on a mud bank.

Due to the large areas of mud exposed between high and low tides, Breydon water and the Lower Broads in general simply teem with wading birds. Flocks of small waders, well dressed oyster catchers in black and white shirts fronts and of course those oddballs of the waterfowl world, the goosanders. The goosanders give the impression that the makers of ducks and geese at the duck and geese making factory decided to use up all the left over bits from the parts bin and create – "well let's call the new model the goosander"

Leaving Breydon water the left hand fork is the mouth of the Waveney – to which I shall return later – whilst the right hand fork – the one near the windmill – is the mouth of the river Yare. Heading up the Yare takes you to Reedham, yet

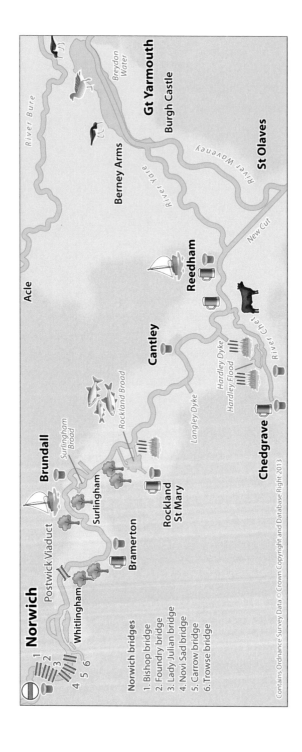

Norwich

Postwick Viaduct

Whitlingham

Brundall

Surlingham

Bramerton

Rockland
St Mary

Surlingham Broad

Rockland Broad

Acle

Cantley

Reedham

River Bure

Berney Arms

Breydon Water

Gt Yarmouth

Burgh Castle

River Yare

New Cut

River Waveney

St Olaves

Langley Dyke

Hardley Dyke

Hardley Flood

Chedgrave

River Chet

Norwich bridges

1. Bishop bridge
2. Foundry bridge
3. Lady Julian bridge
4. Novi Sad bridge
5. Carrow bridge
6. Trowse bridge

again a pleasant picturesque village with a small boatyard (Sanderson's) and a couple of really fine pubs.

This far down the Yare the fishing is OK but does not really get fully into its stride till Cantley. That said the slight salinity of the water on the Lower Yare can turn up surprises with the occasional wayward bass falling to spinning tactics as high as Reedham.

As you leave Reedham you will pass the car ferry which is usually in use. The ferryman will either wave you through or halt you as the case may be. When you do pass keep midway between the back of the ferry and the bank as this will ensure that the slack ferry chain is well submerged.

Joining the Yare past the ferry is the diminutive river Chet. The Chet does not quite ooze the lush rivery charm of some of the smaller tree lined Broads Rivers such as the upper Ant or Waveney. However, as it crooks and hooks past Hardley flood on its wayward path up to Lodden it does have something about it. Perhaps the mud, sky, water and reed collage of the Lower South Broads, only this time executed in miniature.

Back on the OK Yare and the sugar factory at Cantley is never out of sight for a while like a magnificently hideous ugly sister who hogs the pantomime stage. It is on this stretch between Cantley and Brundell that the Yare seems to soften and transforms itself from its impressive lower reaches to its more picturesque upper section.

Rockland broad is connected to the Yare via short dyke at one end and the Fleet at the other. The broad itself is one of those with a navigation running through it marked by posts, with a single branch off the main body of water leading to Rockland Staith. Both Short Dyke and the Fleet fish like a peach particularly where they join the Yare. This far up the river, rudd become more abundant especially in the summer, adding gold to the silver and bronze of roach and bream. As for Rockland broad itself – particularly at the Fleet end – it looks so good that if it could not quite break your heart with a single glance you have the feeling that it might be able to dent it a bit.

Brundell in common with other small broads towns has its marinas and high class riverside developments as you enter. It is also home to Brooms boatyard which builds their own design of slick coupe type craft for sale rather than hire, each costing about the price of a small house.

As you leave Brundell and head up the last leg of the OK Yare to Norwich the river remains very pretty, right up to Postwick viaduct that is after which it all starts to get very urban. If you are travelling on this section at the weekend it is well worth keeping a weather eye out for row boats – sculls, eights that sort of thing – from the busy Norwich rowing club. The thing about rowers is that they have their backs to you and are often concentrating more on their stroke than what they are actually heading for. If what they are heading for is you, get out of the way and do not be afraid to pip your horn to make them aware of your presence. The other thing is to slow down so as not to create too much wash as the narrow sculling boats are not the most stable of craft.

Heading towards the end of the Navigation in Norwich there are at least half a dozen bridges of one sort or another, although none of them are tight even for a large cruiser. The moorings in Norwich are pleasant enough although can get busy as you would expect being in the heart of a city.

The River Waveney

Leaving Breydon water from Yarmouth the left hand fork takes you into the Waveney. The Waveney is unusual

The River Waveney

Gt Yarmouth

River Yare

Reedham

Cantley

Chedgrave

River Yare

River Chet

New Cut

River Waveney

St Olaves Bridge
St Olaves
Herringfleet

Haddiscoe Flyover

Haddiscoe

Somerleyton

Lowestoft

Mutford Bridge

Oulton Dyke

Oulton Broad

River Waveney

Burgh St Peter

Aldeby

Old Bridge
Beccles

New Bridge

Geldeston Dyke
Geldeston

Geldeston Lock

River Waveney

Bungay

amongst rivers in that it has two mouths, the first at Great Yarmouth via Breydon water and the second at Lowestoft by way of Oulton Dyke and Oulton Broad. The Yarmouth Lowestoft section of the Waveny runs fast for a broads river with a fair drop between high and low tides. This is something well worth keeping in mind when mooring on this section. Moor securely but leave plenty of slack on the mooring rope if you tie up at high tide to take account of the fall as the tide goes out.

There is a narrow canal like navigation called new cut that joins this section of the Waveney to the Yare. It is kind of a Great Yarmouth bypass but without the tarmac. There are moorings at St Olaves and also the village of Somerleyton. The countryside around Somerleyton and Fritton is, in high summer, breath takingly beautiful. The village is an estate one with each individual cottage looking like it has been painted into the landscape by Constable, no coincidence there as this is actually Constable country. In June the fields and hedges are a thousand shades of green onto which an occasional kaleidoscope of yellows, whites and blues are projected. Quite honestly it is a stretch of countryside so stunning that it is hard to believe that it is entirely real.

At Somerleyton there are large shoals of really big bream in evidence and in some ways it is reminiscent of Acle on the Bure. As the Waveney runs fast and deep on this section it lends itself to feeder fishing. That said some tactic to counter the soft mud (such as taking the feeder off the mainline via a stiff link) is in order, as the Waveney mud will grab the feeder like a misers hand around a fifty quid note.

Moving up the Waveney from Lowestoft the river transforms from the mud and reed of the lower reaches to well drained pasture. The pasture supports beef cattle, with the un-grazed grass fields usually cut for hay or silage to feed the cattle in winter.

The drainage of the broads was originally achieved by cutting dykes into which tile drains laid beneath the fields ran. The water from these dykes (which are often below sea level) could then be pumped up into the rivers by windmills. Hence the number of abandoned mills on the broads. Today however the fields are drained by a series of automated pumping stations along the lower reaches of each broads river. Whilst the fields are protected from direct flooding by one and in some cases two flood banks. Due to this system of pumps and flood banks land can be farmed that would be below sea level at high tide. The drainage however only goes so far on the broads, with large areas still maintained as floods and reed beds for nature reserves and wildlife. It is a balance that the broads have – in my view- got about right.

Back to those fields of pasture grazed by cattle beside the river. Why pasture? Well down near the rivers heavy clay like soil types predominate Thames and Newchurch series along with Altcarr1 and 11 series soils. All of these soil types found in the valleys near the rivers tend to share similar properties. They are moisture retentive in the summer (aiding grass growth) still prone to occasional flooding and are difficult to work into a fine seed bed for arable crops. These soil types therefore naturally lend themselves to pasture rather than arable.

As you cruise along the broads rivers you will notice that the farmsteads (the farm house, yard and farm buildings) are generally situated on the dryer rises that run up from the rivers with no chance of flooding.

Norfolk is generally known for its lighter soils and low rainfall. Typically 24 inches a year. The light brashy soils that predominate on the rises away from the river are easily worked for arable cropping. They favour the more drought tolerant crops such as sugar beet and barley, which feature in many a Norfolk farms arable rotation. On the broads lighter soils are the Wick 11 and 111 series with the Burlington 111 series between the Yare and the Waveney. On the Suffolk broads are the Beccles 1, 11 and 111 series around – yes you have guessed it –Beccles.

Cruising up to Beccles the river becomes idyllic and by the time you get to Beccles the Waveney has such charm that you can expect to see rat, mole and toad from Wind in the Willows rowing round the next bend towards you.

Beccles itself is well worth a mention for having all the charms of a broads market town and is perhaps the better for being a bit more understated than Wroxham. There are two bridges in Beccles, the first unlikely to have the top off even the largest cruiser, whilst the second lower bridge thins out the boat traffic, making the Upper Waveney accessible only to the smaller craft.

The Waveney beyond Beccles is the sort of river that put the M in meander and it twists and turns like an eel showing off some of its more serpentine moves. The river is also shallower up here and weedy for a broads river, with many of the swims thick with lilies, underwater cabbage and streamer weed. It contains the usual mixed bag of broads fish, with the addition of a good head of chub. If you particularly wish to target chubb then the snaggier swims are plum spots, whilst some bread mixed with primular cheese spread is traditionally considered prime chub fodder.

To widen the net of target species a worm is pretty much a catch all bait. Whilst for silver fish a clear glide where you can trot a float down is probably the number one spot. On the Upper Waveney however you may have to shallow up considerably to run a float through a swim due to the weed. In this situation I would generally dispense with ground bait as a carrier altogether and simply loose feed a steady stream of maggots or casters, to be carried along by the flow.

This section of the Waveney is knee deep in secluded moorings with its many bends and tree lined banks. Ahh paradise one more, or at least some where close.

CHAPTER 2

Fishing on the Broads

When to Fish

Probably the single biggest factor in determining if you are going to catch fish is not the choice of one bait over another, let alone some finer point relating to tackle or terminal rigs, but simply whether the fish are on the feed or not. So where does that leave us with regards to feeding times on the broads? For eels an hour before dawn is often absolutely prime time, predominantly night feeders although they will feed during the day, usually during or after a thunder storm or those dull low pressure, high shower risk days with a bit of a warm feel about them. Bream too fall into the dawn dusk pattern of feeding and the day when they just would not stop biting, to the extent that you got fed up before they did, is usually one where the dawn dusk feeding session is prolonged due to favourable bream weather. It is those dull overcast low pressure, warmish days again.

Silver fish on the other hand particularly Rudd – shoals of which can be found in Barton Broad in the North Broads or Short Dyke off Rockland Broad in the South Broads, seem more tolerant of sunlight on the water and can still keep feeding on a hot summers afternoon. Small perch and that cheeky little demented dwarf of the broads the Tommy Ruff will also feed on those hot lazy days. If you are looking for perch on a hot hang dog day and happen to be on one of those perchy tree lined upper reaches of the Ant or Waveney then a bait cast actually under an overhanging tree is well worth fishing as shoals of small to medium sized perch often seem to congregate beneath these in hot conditions. That said I do feel that bigger perch fall more easily into the dawn dusk feeding cycle.

Having just spent some time emphasising the dawn dusk feeding cycle I would add the caveat that it is perfectly capable of being altered by available food supply either natural or man-made. Thus on a heavily fished section where bait is regularly thrown into the water by anglers between say 9am and 5pm the fish obviously respond to this readily available feast by modifying their feeding times.

Extreme examples of this are the heavily stocked commercial fisheries where the fish become almost completely reliant on introduced food and the opening of the gates at 8 o'clock in the morning more or less indicates feeding time. In such waters a disturbance overhead far from spooking the fish as it would their more fearful cousins that swim in natural waters, actually indicates to the commercial fish the introduction of feed overhead which they then try to intercept high in the water spurred into this behaviour by competition with their fellows. This has led to the bizarre "splash em" technique on commercial fisheries where anglers when not actually introducing feed aim to simulate the splash of feed entering the water by slapping the surface with their pole tips in order to exploit the association in the fishes mind between the splash and feeding time.

How strong the stimulus of artificial food is in changing behaviour can perhaps be glimpsed by comparing the effort necessary for a fish to gain a meal from sifting say hundreds of tiny blood worms with that of the easily available plenty laid out by the angler.

The biggest mistake in fishing – and it is a hotly contested prize – is simply to go fishing on a nice day and then pack up just before the fish really get to feeding at dusk. I am taking a nice day here to mean high pressure blue skies, bright sunshine etc. Although this is perhaps one of the great pleasures of fishing and boating on the broads, that the hot days are just about ideal for messing about, cruising in the boat and other forms of holidaying in general.

When it comes to time of year, early season fishing where you are waiting for the water temperature to rise and trigger the fish into spring feeding mode does not really apply to the broads as it is closed season until June 16th by which time the fish have long ago shaken off their winter torper. Similarly with the possible exception of pike, the rapid fall in temperature after the end of September generally leads to a considerable slowing in fish feeding activity. Bream as a general rule are a summer species as are rudd although the roach will shoal up quite tightly in the right place in the colder months and continue to feed if you catch them on the right day. Mariners often fish well in the winter as the water can be slightly warmer from the boats running their engines. Sometimes the right day in winter can be almost the opposite of the right day in summer as peak feeding time can be around mid-day to early afternoon on a day when there is some sunlight penetrating the water to stimulate the fish. That said most yards take their boats out of the water at the end of October as the bookings start to fall off in the Autumn so the cruising/fishing season falls together quite neatly in that mid-June to early October slot.

Fishing on the Broads
Rods and Reels

A basic medium feeder rod is probably the most useful rod to have. It needs to be capable of handling 5lbs. plus bream in a strong current and the odd good eel and believe me the good eels of the broads can be extremely odd – it's all that swimming backwards shaking their heads when hooked that does it. If you are into test curves 1.25– 1.5 lbs. is about right. A feeder rod that comes with an alternative Avon tip such as those popularised by that well known Norfolk angler John Wilson is ideal as it can double up as a float rod at any time. In my view a real pig of a river feeder rod like those used for barble on the Severn and Trent is rather over egging it on the broads.

The dominant broads species such as bream and roach are not by their nature savage biting fish, so a bait runner reel is not really necessary, although use one if you have one by all means. A simple 4000 series fixed spool reel loaded with 5 or 6lbs. mono is about right in my view. The river fishing aficionados may refuse to leave home without their beloved centerpin reels and these are extremely pleasant to use and are the classic reels for trotting.

For Pike fishing although the broads pike can be big you are generally fishing within twenty to thirty yards of the boat so a light pike/carp rod of 2 -2.5lbs. test curve with a forgiving action is my own preference. However most anglers would prefer a beefier stick with a 3-3.5 lb. test curve well capable of lugging out fairly hefty dead baits. A 4000 – 6000 series fixed spool reel loaded with an 8lb plus mono is a suitable set up. Some pike anglers prefer to use a more expensive braided mainline although its low diameter anti stretch advantages are arguably less relevant for boat fishing than bank fishing in large waters.

Boat Fishing Gadgets

Gadgets are – by their nature unnecessary but nice and occasionally even useful to own. Here are a couple of those small objects of desire for boat fishing.

A rod rest that clamps onto the boat, – these are relatively inexpensive and really are a handy little gadget. A float for the landing net is also a good idea as landing nets do seem particularly prone to being blown off the roof of the boat or simply dropped into the water whilst netting a fish by an unusually kak handed angler. (Important authoritorial note) ★ I really must get a net float having lost yet another landing net last year.

That said when it comes to packing your fishing stuff it is well worth remembering that fishing tackle is the most addictive substance known to man, with the possible exception of Pringles and heroin, so how about taking it easy and lightening the load.

Baits for the Broads

Where do you stand on eels? What are your politics when it comes to the eel –Anguilla anguilla? This is a key question on the broads, particularly on overcast showery days, early mornings, and evenings or more particularly at night when the eel population of the broads are on the prowl. What they are on prowl for is any meat based feed. They will nibble dead bait put out for pike, wolf a piece of luncheon meat and maggots and worms are their bread and butter.

If you are in the eel fan club – and personally I am a paid up member – then a good basic approach to bait is a fishmeal based ground bait such as a halibut based method mix, to which a leavening of loose maggots is added. To try and pick up the better fish a small red worm or dendrobaena does seem to have a premium over maggots as a hook bait. This approach will catch pretty much anything that swims in the broads. bream, roach, rudd, hybrids, eels, perch and the occasional pike who usually take the worm on the retrieve – perhaps mistaking it for a bootlace eel – and not forgetting of course those greedy little dwarfs of the broads the over ambitious Tommys trying to gorge themselves on a worm probably half their own size. In short this is a type of fishing and bait combination where you never know what is going to turn up next.

Baits to Target Bream and Silver Fish

If on the other hand you profess either an aversion to eels or simply wish to target bream and silver fish exclusively then your best bet is for a sweet biscuit type ground bait such as "sweet Breams" or a sweet carp mix with hemp and particles. Incidentally if you wish to know if a particular ground bait is sweet or fishmeal based, give it a sniff. To keep the cost down on your ground bait a simple bulk bag of brown crumb still has a place and may be particularly relevant if you wish to introduce large quantities of feed into a broad to attract one of the really immense shoals of bream. A tin of hemp is a good attractor to mix with your ground bait (boil up your own if you want to save on cost) as are a few casters which bream absolutely love.

If you are targeting bream more particularly than the silver fish then a larger more selective bait combination has its place. In this situation sweetcorn really comes into its own both mixed with the ground bait and fished on the hook. Personally if the bream are really biting that is when I would change to corn on the hook as it does seem to pick out the better sized fish. As a final bait in this situation do not discount bread flake. Still a good bait particularly where neutral buoyancy is an advantage for example on a soft silty bottom. In fast flowing water a fresh, doughy, stodgy white bread is an advantage to retaining the flake on the hook for longer.

Baits to Target Perch and Eels

If you wish to specifically target eels and good sized fish then straight maggots can be used in the feeder, or mixed into a minimum of ground bait combined with a large worm on the hook such as a dendrobaena or lob. I am a particular fan of this bait combination where good sized perch are numerous such as on the Upper Ant or Upper Waveney, although it can also be used to pick out specimen bream, silver fish and eels all along the broads system. It is always worth a slow retrieve when fishing this method as this seems to particularly appeal to predatory fish such as pike and perch.

Feeder Fishing

Having outlined different ground bait and hook bait combinations to target different species this rather begs the question, how best to fish them? Feeder fishing is an extremely proficient method of getting the hook bait and ground bait to the fish together. In fast flowing river currents this is particularly problematic as the current washes away the free offerings. However in feeder fishing – all things being equal – as your hook bait and ground bait are tethered together at most a few feet apart, it is practically a bomb proof method of getting your hook bait and ground bait working together to catch fish.

The middle and lower reaches of the Broads Rivers run swiftly – both ways depending on the tide – and in this situation a closed feeder comes into its own to get the ground bait down onto the river bed. In strong currents it's often better to mix the ground bait quite stodgy as this aids its retention in the feeder. A roll of electrical tape is also a useful thing to have in the tackle box as it can be wrapped round the feeder to close off some of the holes and cut down the rate at which the ground bait is washed from the feeder in fast flows.

With this type of feeder fishing where you are not looking to pick up fish on the drop, but rather to pin your bait to the bottom, hook lengths tend to be short. Two to three feet is probably a good average at which to start. After a couple of hours fishing it is often worth doubling the hook length for a few casts as there may well be bigger fish feeding that are hanging back from the feeder in the way that wary bigger fish will.

"A simple ledger link set up. This rig will catch pretty much anything that swims in the broads, roach, bream, perch and even the odd eel".

When fishing a closed feeder you are a bit limited on what you can put into your ground bait as sweetcorn or whole worms for example are usually larger than the holes in the feeder and so are not washed out by the current. These baits if they are to be introduced are therefore best incorporated in a ball or two of stodgy ground bait thrown well up the flow to where the feeder is being cast.

The closed feeder filled with maggots fished with a large worm on the hook can be an absolute nailer for eels as an enticing trickle of maggots squirm their way out of the feeder. As a quick aside, whilst keeping maggots in a cool environment does increase their usable life before they turn to casters I do believe in letting maggots heat up to the extent that they get a "sweat on" for an hour or so before fishing. If you follow this procedure a quick sniff will confirm how the maggoty smell has been intensified by sweating the maggots and I believe that the stench is extremely attractive to fish, particularly eels.

In feeder fishing whether using a closed or open type feeder it is often advisable to make several casts in quick succession initially, in order to introduce a quantity of bait into the swim and there after play it by ear, depending on whether fish and bites are forthcoming. In reasonable conditions a good sized feeder of say 2 inches in length with a 50gram weight would be suitable for most broads rivers, although you may wish to dispense with some of the weight in the Broads themselves, particularly those that have soft muddy bottoms.

If open ended cage type feeders are used in fast flowing water the majority of the ground bait is usually washed out by the current as it sinks to the river bed. A pattern of feed is therefore produced with ground bait and feed suspended in the current as it is washed along with the flow. This is not necessarily a bad thing and in this situation the hook bait is best fished on a long hook length – six foot plus is not too much. Hook bait that tends towards neutral buoyancy – such as well-turned casters or bread flake will be held in the flow of the current for longer.

"A simple ledger link again but this time set up more with bream in mind".

In the slower upper reaches of the Broads Rivers or in the broads themselves the open ended feeder in conjunction with a long hook length and slow sinking baits will pick up fish on the drop. When fishing this technique mixing your ground bait semi dry will create a cloud of ground bait as the feeder hits the water. Having said this I would still suggest that the more standard hook length of around three feet fished with bigger hook baits such as worm or sweetcorn on the bottom will consistently produce the better fish.

Rigs for Feeder Fishing

The straight forward ledger link is in my view as good a rig as any for the broads. Its two great strengths are its simplicity and its versatility. If you want to tweak it a bit then a match type hook link can be used for bream and silver fish. These lines are very supple, stretchy and have a low diameter for their breaking strain. For eel fishing if you want to use a separate hook length material then this is where the stiff anti tangle characteristics of a material like fluorocarbon come into their own, as eels are particularly adept at transforming the straightest of hook lengths into the most impenetrable of slimy knots. However having looked at two separate hook length materials in this as in all aspects of fishing it is easy to overcomplicate. So applying this to hook links there is nothing wrong with using your mainline straight through and if it gets slimed and tangled by an eel – well cut off the kinked section, move the feeder up the line and tie on a new hook. Simple.

A feeder rig for a river with a soft silty bottom. A stiff anti-tangle hook length such as I.Q. is a good idea with this type of rig.

There are however situations on the broads where in my view it does pay to deviate from the straight forward ledger link set up. Soft bottoms – as you will know if you suffer from one yourself – can be a problem. In many of the broads and some of the stretches of rivers such as the Somerleyton/ Fritton section of the Waveney soft silty bottoms just grab the feeder, negating the free running properties of the ledger link. In such a situation you will find that the feeder needs a good yuk to free it from the suction of the silt and will be covered in muddy detritus on the retrieve.

In still water situations this would usually be countered by attaching the feeder to the end of the mainline whilst taking the hook length off the mainline via a swivel, thus allowing it to "helicopter" around the mainline to use a modern rig type term. In this situation a stiff anti tangle hook length can be used in conjunction with a neutral buoyancy bait thus stopping the bait sinking into the sediment. This set up used to be called a paternoster in fishing books and is sort of half way to a chod rig but without the pop up bait.

A rig for soft silty bottoms, this time fished in a broad

My own view on this approach is that although I have used it in running water I do not think that it naturally lends itself to presenting the hook bait down the flow of the current along with the ground bait and loose feed washed from the feeder. I also tend to view a freer running rig as the best option for the shyer biting species of the broads such as bream and silver fish. For these reasons I therefore favour the path less travelled and adapt the ledger link by taking the feeder off the mainline via a swivel and stiff link or even a light boom if you are inclined to try and prevent tangles. If you do not have a stiff link material in your tackle box a length of heavy mono which can be doubled up if necessary to form a loop can help to keep the feeder link from wrapping itself around the mainline.

Float Fishing

There are some things in life that are just pleasant to do and float fishing is one of them. Ok it's not a heady rush of excitement, I grant you, but it's like watching the waves break on the sea shore – hypnotic.

You can split float fishing into trotting and fishing static. Looking at trotting first, you are introducing feed into the head of the swim with each cast (and it is this regular feeding that is one of the great secrets of trotting) as the feed is carried along by the current it falls to the river bed, where in a strong current it continues to be washed down stream. What you are aiming to do is present your baited hook quite naturally in this stream of falling food. It is always worth keeping this underwater picture in your mind's eye when setting up a rig on a particular swim. For example if the current is flowing fast you will need a bigger river float such as a chubber or avon to ride the water, with more shot bunched down towards the hook to make your bait

Stick float fishing on a shallow glide

fall through the water if you want to fish at any depth. Conversely on shallower sections with less flow a smaller stick float shotted shirt button fashion (i.e.: a series of small shot regularly spaced down the line) really comes into its own.

As a general rule on the broads most of the main rivers tend to be a bit too deep and fast for fishing a delicate stick float to advantage. Yet occasionally – just occasionally in this world perfection exists – that peach of a shallow glide stacked full of fish and not another soul in sight.

A rig to float fish in a swim that runs fast and deep

Having just eulogized about trotting a light stick float on the upper reaches of the broads system do not be afraid to get a big chubber or avon float out of the box on a swim that makes a metaphysical poet look shallow and runs like a steam train. When you are fishing this sort of swim it usually pays to mix the feed fairly stiff and stodgy to try and get it down to some fish before it is washed out of your swim by the current.

As with all trotting the key along with regular feeding is to keep in close and constant contact with your float by regularly picking the bow of line that forms in the current up off the water and placing it behind the float. If you get really trick at this you may start greasing you line with a floatant and even have a separate centre pin reel for trotting (by this time you may start to think yourself as being pretty proficient at this old trotting lark.) But hey, your normal fixed spool reel fished bail arm open and controlling the line peeling off the spool with your index finger as the float runs down the swim works almost as well. By the way, holding your float hard back occasionally, particularly at the tail end of your swim, causing the bait to rise up in the current is one of those small left handed bits of wisdom which can often glean you a few extra bites.

Waggler Fishing and Fishing Static

Another path in float fishing is to use that most versatile of all floats the waggler. For rivers a fairly buoyant float is often needed, traditionally a thick tipped peacock quill although more commonly now perhaps a stubby foam or balsa, pellet waggler. Although initially designed as still water floats for carp in commercial fisheries, thick pellet wagglers are ideal for running water as they ride the current like a cork in a washing machine.

Float fishing rig for perch and eels

Where the waggler really comes into its own is on the broads themselves which are generally shallow – 5-7 feet being about the norm with a soft muddy bottom. Hardly ideal for feeder fishing. In this situation the light touch of waggler fishing is practically unbeatable for presenting a bait deftly on top of silt or mud. A slightly less buoyant waggler such as a fine crystal is probably first choice here depending on the amount of chop on the water.

Fishing static on running water (stret pegging) is best suited to the upper reaches of the Broads Rivers such as the Ant, Thurne or Waveney. What is needed is a big float and plenty of shot to hold the bottom. The further out into the flow you fish the greater the drag on the line, so it is a technique that comes into its own quite tight to the banks. If you are into eeling – yes back to my old friends again – then a bulbous bobbin type float and a real python of a worm fished into the darkness are an absolutely nailing combination.

As a parting curved ball when float fishing in running water it is not a daft plan to cast out over depth with not quite enough weight down the line to hold the bottom in full flow. Then see where your bait ends up just holding the bottom as these havens of slack water often hold surprisingly good fish, particularly if the river is in flood. Similarly when fishing a bend look for the crease where the fast water runs against the slow causing natural food to fall out of suspension, as this too is often a plum spot for your bait.

Pike Fishing on the Broads

If you want to find the hunter – look for the hunted. Pretty much anywhere and everywhere on the broads contain pike – and pike will patrol considerable distances for food – it is just that higher densities of pike are drawn by higher densities of fodder fish. So places like Candle Dyke and Heigham Sound are natural hotspots for pike, due in large part to the sheer quantity of bream, roach and hybrid shoals that they contain.

It is also worth turning over another card and saying that pike thrive on neglect – possibly due to an increased mortality rate amongst caught pike even when treated with care and returned. It is also worth noting that people who have tried to create commercial pike fisheries by stocking large quantities of surplus fish from fish farms as prey have generally met with very little success. Whilst those fishery owners who do not even want pike present, let alone wish to encourage them, have often (unwittingly in the case of put and take trout reservoirs) produced some superb pike waters. That it is not only the density of prey fish in the trout fisheries on which the pike thrive but also the neglect is a conclusion which is hard to escape.

Returning to Candle Dyke on Heigham Sound the proximity of large areas that can provide at least a partial refuge for pike in the form of Martham broad and to a lesser extent Hickling and Horsey (there is a voluntary ban on powered craft in Horsey during the winter by the way) probably helps to contribute to the density of pike. It is also worth noting that Candle Dyke and Heigham Sound form a natural bottle neck between the Horsey, Hickling area and the Thurne which may also serve to funnel pike into this area. On the subject of the creation of refuge areas, whilst legislation naturally tends to grate upon my soul like a saw blade drawn across my fingers, no pleasure craft/no fishing areas such as Martham Broad do, in my view, contribute rather than detract from the fishing. Less is sometimes more, or at least better.

Whilst discussing pike densities a thought also worth bearing in mind is the relationship between any species and it's food supply. Imagine for one moment the vast abundance of daphnia, blood worms and other natural food needed to support a single roach and then cast that same dice again and picture the numerous roach needed to support a single pike. So that even in a rich natural habitat such as the broads the capture of every individual pike should be appreciated for what it is – a gift from the tip of natures pyramid.

Lure Fishing for Pike

When it comes to the choice of lure it is worth keeping in mind that the broads themselves are generally shallow, 5-7 feet being about the norm. Consequently when fishing spoons, something light like a small ABU toby is more the order of the day rather than a deep fishing heavy spoon. Similarly when fishing a conventional hard bodied plug a floater or slow sinker is often the best choice. On a day when there is some warmth to the water I have great faith in that old stager of a red head with a white or silver body. That said a nailing pattern one day can be a complete dud the next, depending on – well, either a whole host of scientific factors not easily comprehensible to the lay person, or merely the caprice of the pike headed god of the broads, depending entirely upon you philosophy.

For soft bodied lures it is much the same story with heavily weighted shads generally fishing too deep for the majority of the broads. My own preferences in soft bodied lures are naturalistic types such as roach or eel patterns, with bulbous tails, that wag like over enthusiastic springer spaniels.

As a last word on lure fishing there is generally no need to strike as the pike usually hook themselves against the momentum of the retrieve.

Dead Baiting for Pike

When it comes to dead baiting for pike I am a fan of getting some movement into the bait. A bait fished hard on the bottom will certainly catch pike – particularly when they are more slothful in the winter months. However I do believe that a static bait makes pike fishing – a waiting game at the best of times – still slower.

Using the current to impart movement into a dead bait on a fast flowing river

With this in mind when ledgering hard on the bottom occasionally lift the rod with a couple of turns of the reel handle, this will pick the bait up in the water and then cause it to flutter enticingly back onto the riverbed. Even a light twitch of the bait every minute or so can catch the eye of a passing predator and trigger a feeding response. Having said this for running water a rig that keeps the dead bait flashing silver in the current is in my view a real winner.

Perhaps the simplest way to impart this movement into the dead bait is to trot it through the swim beneath a large pike float, holding it back occasionally to lift the bait in the water. However my own preference if there is a strong flow is to put a lump of lead down the line sufficient to hold the bottom and then take the snap tackle off the mainline (via a three way swivel or light boom to stop it twisting around the mainline if you are in a technical mood). In a good flow this will keep a light bait wafting and waving in the current.

In still water situations such as the broads where this rig is not usually practicable you can drift a bait if there is some chop or tow on the water. Alternatively pop a bait up off the bottom on a short link with the aid of a polystyrene ball or two in order to achieve the necessary buoyancy.

Pike Care

Catching a pike is one thing, unhooking it quite another – it is that mouthful of teeth that tends to put people off. Personally I do believe that pike may be much more susceptible to damage than one might imagine from looking at the scaly exterior of the toothy Leviathans. Besides if you have been blessed with the pikely bounty of the broads, you owe it to your captive to treat it right. When you first part the folds of the landing net if you have a thrasher on your hands – and it will be obvious if you have – resist the temptation to wrestle it into submission a' la Johnny Wisemuller in his role as Tarzan. Instead take a wet cloth or towel and throw it over the pike's head and upper body for a few moments and nine times out of ten it will lie still. Kneel down with your knees astride the pike and roll the fish onto it's back. Then slip two fingers into the pikes lower gill and prize open the bottom of the jaw. You will now be looking into a mouthful of teeth and down the gullet of the pike. In this position, gazing up at you with its lower jaw held open the pike will find it quite impossible to bite. Now clip a strong pair of long nosed forceps onto the treble hook and attempt to remove it. Sometimes it is easier to cut the wire trace with pliers and remove the treble via the gill rakes.

When unhooking pike I wear light leather gloves (although some fishermen prefer a chain mail butcher's glove) heavy work gloves are too cumbersome for what is in essence quite a delicate operation.

I am sure I recognise that smile.

I am now going to deal with a difficult topic, which is what to do if a pike is really deeply hooked and by this I mean what if the trebles are well out of sight? As in all things prevention is better than cure – so strike earlier rather than later when you have a bite, Oh and do not leave your rod unattended. With the best will in the world you will occasionally be faced with a deep hooked fish. This can happen in all forms of fishing, whatever the quarry and eels in particular do seem particularly prone to bolting the bait, hook and all beyond the reach of the disgorger. In this situation I would give a slow yet fairly firm pull on the line. If this does not succeed in freeing the hook then I would cut the line and return the fish. As a simple country boy I would much prefer in this situation to knock the fish on the head and pan fry it for supper. However these days it is strictly catch and release even if on the odd occasion it causes the fish more suffering in the long run – but then that is politics for you.

CHAPTER 3

Boating on the Broads

Day Hire and Day Tripping

Pretty much all towns and villages on the broads have some sort of connection to boating, from the simplest village staith to extensive marinas. If you have your own trailer sailor there are plenty of public slipways. Alternatively there are no shortage of day boat hire firms such as Phoenix Hire at Potter Higham. What you usually get is a launch type boat with an out board motor, more often than not these days an electric out board – clean quiet and easy to start. You can also hire an open decked tender type rowing boat with a pair of oars or in the case of canoes, paddles. In fact the flat bottomed Native American canoe experience has become one of the most popular ways to explore the quieter broads in recent years.

Another popular way of getting afloat on the wet stuff and one which seems particularly favoured by the more elderly day trippers is the river boat trip. These can vary from the eco-friendly solar powered Ra sun boat of Barton Broad, to the garish Mississippi paddle boat moored up at Wroxham.

On the subject of slightly out of the ordinary boats on the broads it is worth making the point that historically narrow boats or canal boats as they are often called were never really a feature of the broads. The river currents particularly round Yarmouth and Lowestoft tends to run too fast for traditional narrow boats. What the broads had instead was the Norfolk Wherry which is a broad bottomed cargo sail boat, similar in many ways to the keels or slops found on other river systems in the UK. There are some beautifully restored Norfolk Wherrys that still sail, usually crewed by a select and dedicated band of middle aged men who take part annually in Norfolk's bushiest beard competition and who mark each sailing trip by consuming enough real ale to float a yacht.

A Richardsons Classic. In this case Serene Gem

Holiday Hire

Starting up at Stalham is the Richardson's yard; theirs is probably the biggest fleet on the broads offering something for everyone. The Richardson classic design is essentially long low and almost barge like. The advantage to this type of craft is the low air draft which makes the charmed upper reaches of the Broads Rivers, beyond the low bridges accessible to you. In fact when hiring any boat it is always well worth asking which bridges it will or will not pass under. Richardson's also have what they call their platinum class cruisers moored at their Moonfleet yard at Stalham. This is the up market end of the fleet. There is also a small Richardson's yard at Acle.

Barnes Brinkcraft of Wroxham are a friendly – mind you they are all friendly in Norfolk, it must be something they put in the water – family run boatyard. They have a fleet of around thirty five modern and well maintained cruisers. Royalls boatyard also at Wroxham is another well established class act in boat hire with a broads history going back over the generations. Just down the river at Horning is Posh Boats with a small fleet of – well the name says it all – posh boats. This seems to be something of a theme at Horning with Le Boat also specialising in the up market and to be quite honest Le Boat offer some of the best turned out craft for hire on the broads.

Up in Potter Heigham is Herbert Woods catering for the modern cruiser hire market and if you are thinking of buying a second hand boat yourself then Herbert Woods is as good a place to look as any with a wide selection always in stock. Just up from Potter Heigham is Martham Boats whose hire fleet is all wood, with both sailing and cruising models. Their cruisers are their own designed and built J class. The Jayne being the smallest and progressing up through the Janet, Judith and the Juliette. Quite frankly I am a bit of a fan of these boats and the Martham team typifies all that is best about the small friendly Norfolk boat yards. Whilst on the subject of Norfolk folk Terry who shows you how to operate the boats at Martham has an act so good he should be on the tv. After all it cannot be easy keeping your sense of humour when dealing with the general public day in and day out. Particularly when trying to turn someone who may never have even been on a boat in their life into a half competent inland waterways skipper after only a couple of hours tuition. Not only do the Martham team do it as well as anyone they also do it with some of the prettiest wooden boats and to cap it all their prices are extremely reasonable.

Although not a book on sailing I cannot leave the boat hire companies on the North Broads without mentioning the Hunters yard at Horse shoe fen, Ludham. They offer the real 1930's sail boat experience, no fiberglass just wood, no motor just canvas – complete with paraffin lamps and primus stove. One for the purists perhaps?

On the South Broads there are a couple of small yards, Sandersons at Reedham on the Yare and also Pacific Cruisers at Lodden on the small River Chet. Further up the Yare at Brundell are Swancraft which are a quality fleet fitted out at a comparable standard to the Le Boat fleet.

The author, Miss Richards & terrier on a J class wooden cruiser from Martham Boats

Boats – How to Drive and Moore the Things

The Controls

Boats do not as a rule have gears. They are either in gear – in which case the prop shaft turns – or out of gear, in which case the engine will rev but the prop shaft remains stationary. This is usually referred to as pin in (in gear) and pin out (out of gear). On most boats there is actually a pin or button to push to engage the prop shaft next to the throttle. Aha the throttle. This is generally a hand operated lever. Push it forward and you will go forward (assuming that you are in gear, pin in) push it forward some more and you still go forward only faster as the engine revs higher.

Tick over is usually in the central throttle position so if you are pin out (out of gear) you are in neutral with the engine idling. If you then engage the drive (pin in) and pull the throttle backwards you will go backwards. Again as you pull back on the throttle more the higher the engine will rev and the faster you will be travelling in reverse.

Steering is more often than not via a wheel although on narrow boats tillers are still the norm. Brakes. None of those I am afraid on a boat, so to stop you pull the throttle back into reverse, this will slow and then stop the boat. If you stay in reverse you will of course start to travel backwards. To stop the engine a pull stop is most popular which cuts off the fuel.

Casting Off

So much for the controls, what about getting started? Put the boat in neutral (pin out) with some revs on the throttle. When cold most diesels need some pre heating. One turn of the key for 30 seconds to a minute is normal although the instructor at the boatyard will run through the starting procedure. If the boat is slow to start give it some more heat rather than simply churning the motor over and flattening the battery. Oh and most common mistake – trying to start the boat with the pull stop out.

When you are started cast the bow and stern ropes off, then pin in (in gear) and you are away. Coil the mooring ropes up neatly on deck, particularly the stern rope as if this falls into the water and trails behind it is prone to getting snagged up in the prop shaft with interesting results.

If you are leaving a particularly crowded mooring where you are nose to tail without sufficient room to steer the boat out, use the boat hook to push the bow away from the bank and into open water. Sometimes you will find yourself in a tight spot, in a village staithe or a narrow cut with only very limited room to turn the boat around. In this situation many boaters end up thrashing about trying to execute a twenty point turn with much toing, froing and churning of the waters. In just such a situation I well remember a Norfolk old boy saying to me "swing it round on the bow-rope boy". With the boat in neutral let the crew member on the bank push the boat out at one end, then walk up the bank to swing it round on the other rope. It works like a charm.

Mooring Up

A quick word at this point on reversing the boat. You will generally find that a boat is less responsive when reversing. You can still steer but it is going to take it's time to respond. There is a reason for this – when you are cruising forward the prop shaft is pushing water over the rudder improving the steering. When you take the revs off you tend to lose the steering or at least most of it. Ok then, so how do you steer the boat when reversing or idling forward? The answer is basically slowly. The best method is to point your boat roughly in the direction that you intend to go before you put it into reverse or idle. So if you are in a situation where you want to moor end on (many of the busy waterside pubs are stern only mooring to maximise the number of boats they can cater for) the best method is to align the boats stern with the intended mooring whilst in forward. Then reverse straight back. Sometimes wind/current/pure incompetence can cause you to make a hash of any mooring first time around and if it takes a couple of attempts well – where is the rush? After all you are on holiday.

Ok, so what about plain old side on mooring? As nine times out of ten this is the method that you will use. The best wrinkle here is that if there is a current, moor into it. There is a reason for this. As you approach the mooring at a shallow angle, slow down – your steering will lessen but you will continue on the same course into the mooring – then just before the bows bump the bank go into reverse which will bring you virtually to a standstill as you nuzzle up to the mooring. A member of your crew (it is good being skipper as you can quite legitimately refer to any other person on the boat wife, small child, acquaintance etc as your crew) can then step ashore, holding both bow and stern ropes. As they hold or secure the bow rope the current will tend to push the stern gently into the bank. Hence the advantage of always trying to moor into the wind/current.

If for any reason you end up having to moor with the current the flow will tend to swing the stern away from the bank, resulting in the crew member on shore having to hold or haul the stern gently into the mooring on the rope before tying up. Personally on a wide stretch of river with a good flow I would always prefer to use the river to turn into the current if possible, as this does make things so much easier.

In the previous paragraph I mentioned tying the boat up. But to what? And how? Most common on the quay are short mooring posts. Tie up to these with a round turn and a couple of hitches dropped over the top of the post, or alternatively a boatman's hitch. Sometimes instead of posts you get mooring rings, in which case you can either pass the rope through the ring and back onto the boat tying off onto the cleat on the deck, or tie straight to the ring with a round turn and two half hitches. Describing knots on the page never really comes across, so if you are unfamiliar with your hitches, best bet is to get the instructor who shows you round the boat to demonstrate or have a look on You Tube.

If there are no posts and rings for mooring it is time to get the land anchors out, all hire boats come equipped with these and they are essentially hooks with rings on the end that hammer into the bankside.

Highway Code for Rivers

Cruising is all very continental as you get to drive on the right. There are also speed limits on the broads, although there are no speedometers on the boats. An interesting one this. On narrow stretches of the river the limit is usually 3mph increasing to the heady speeds of 4 and even 5mph on the wider lower reaches. The rev counter on the boat is not much help either as at any given revs your speed can vary considerably, depending on whether you are travelling with or against the current. However if your bow waves lap heavily against the bank you are travelling too fast and need to slow down. On busier sections going with the general flow of boat traffic is appropriate. My own view is that the faster you travel the faster the holiday seems to go; it is a time relativity thing and I prefer those long lazy days.

A general rule when cruising is always give way to sail. If a yacht is tacking from side to side in front of you on the river, slow down and pass on the right when they are near the left hand bank. More often than not a yacht will wave you through at the appropriate time. Another common courtesy when cruising is to give anglers plenty of room when passing. Move well over to the center of the river and keep the wash down.

When you pick up the boat it is wise to enquire about the air draft as this can save any unfortunate incidents with low bridges, many boats have a canopy that you can lower if things look a bit tight. As you approach a bridge there is a gauge in the water giving its clearance and this can vary considerably with tide. There are no locks or tunnels on the broads, so no problems there.

Life Afloat

When you pick up the boat you can ask for a short driving lesson on the river, however, more experienced boaters are generally just given a quick run-down on the appliances and controls. It is generally a wise move to check the engine oil, water and also clean out the weed filter if you have been cruising for any length of time on the previous day. If your boat overheats nine times out of ten it will be the weed filter clogged and the engine may need a top up with water. Always let the engine cool right down before checking or topping up with water.

The broads are very boat friendly and many public moorings have bins for rubbish and a tap to take on fresh water. The charge for this is usually a pound dropped into a tin. Depending on the boat you may need to do this every couple of days. The most common mistake when taking on water – filling the diesel tank with H2O, so double check.

Pump outs may be necessary at least once on a holiday and most boat yards will carry this out for a small charge. The diesel tanks should be brim full when you pick the boat up although you may need a refill if you do a lot of cruising. Most boats rely on a dip stick rather than a fuel gauge.

The heaters on hire boats range from the decidedly dicky to the surprisingly good, depending on model. Power for the heaters and lights come from a separate set of batteries to the engine so there is no need to worry about draining them. Hot water is heated via the engine so if you want a shower in the morning you may have to run the engine for a while.

Boating – What can possibly go wrong?

If a person or dog goes overboard the most important thing to remember is to keep them well out of the way of the propeller. Having just fallen into the water someone is obviously having a bad day and slicing them up with the propeller shaft is not going to do anything to improve it. So motor up to them slowly – then pin out disengage the prop. Next throw out the life ring that all boats carry. Boats also generally come with a rope ladder for getting the drowned rat once more aboard.

On the subject of safety equipment provided with the boat the life jackets are often the cumbersome, bright orange, Mitchelin Man type design. To be honest most boaters do not spend their entire holiday cocooned in the bright orange Mr Blobby jacket provided. If you can swim like a fish then fair enough, if you swim like a breeze block then perhaps not so wise. Falling into the latter category I tend to wear a light buoyancy padded waistcoat whilst afloat, although the self-inflating neck scarf type are also popular and even

Swimming is strictly prohibited on the broads, drowning on the other hand is entirely permissable. Here the author demonstrates the art of drowning

less obtrusive to wear. You will have to buy your own I am afraid but in my view it is a few quid well spent.

If you travel with a dog you should consider a canine life jacket. Once again these are relatively inexpensive. When dogs fall into the water they usually either swim after the boat or paddle to the bank where they can experience difficulties getting ashore. I have spent quite a bit of time cruising with terrier and on most holidays she would usually contrive to fall in on at least a couple of occasions. We once lost her for several hours in the vast reed beds of the Upper Thurne with only a rough idea to within a couple of miles where she had fallen in. Luckily this story had a happy ending and we eventually found her on a little reed island towards night fall.

Grounding the boat out is another common problem and usually occurs when you are moored up and the tide goes out leaving you stranded. Leaving some slack on the mooring ropes is often wise as it allows the boat to follow the tide out. If you are left high and dry for any reason and a quick shift or two from forward to reverse does not do the trick, then try pushing away from the bank with the boat hook. If on the other hand you are in the middle of a broad then rocking the boat side to side is worth a try. If all else fails you can either ask for a tow from a passing boat or wait for the tide to come in again and float you off.

If you are cruising along and suddenly start to feel a juddering or thumping from the stern, what you have probably done is fouled up the prop shaft. If it is just a plastic bag or something similar then going from forward to reverse sharply a couple of times will often clear the obstruction. If on the other hand it is – for example a length of nylon rope – then you may have to moor up and ring the boatyard who will send someone out to remove the offending artefact.

At the end of the day boats do on occasions breakdown. In the event of a breakdown proceed as follows – moor up, call the boatyard and let them deal with it. This allows you to do one of the following 1) read a good book, 2) go for a walk or have a nosey round the local market town or village, 3) get the rods out and you never know you might even catch a few.

Thanks for reading. Take it easy and good times or what you will from Peter Craven. Scawby, Lincolnshire 2013.